WHEN JESUS WAS BORN

MARYANN J. DOTTS

Illustrated by Tom Armstrong

Abingdon Press
Nashville

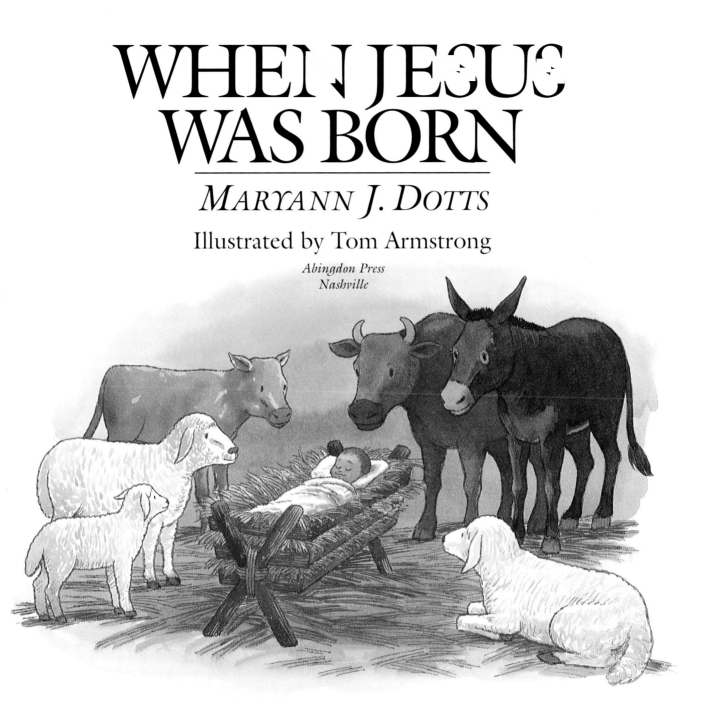

When Jesus Was Born

Library of Congress Cataloging-in-Publication Data

Dotts, Maryann J.
  When Jesus was born / Maryann J. Dotts ; illustrated by Tom Armstrong.
    p.   cm.
  ISBN 0-687-02004-2   (pbk. : alk. paper)
    1. Jesus Christ—Nativity—Juvenile literature.   2. Bible stories, English—N.T. Gospels.   [1. Jesus Christ—Nativity.   2. Bible stories—N.T.]   I. Armstrong, Tom, ill.   II. Title.
BT315.2.D67   1994
232.92—dc20   93-49667

95 96 97 98 99 00 01 02 — 10 9 8 7 6 5 4

MANUFACTURED IN MEXICO

To Parents—
The First Teachers of Religion

Notes to Adults

Share *When Jesus Was Born* with the child(ren) as a preparation for the Advent and Christmas seasons.

The emphasis in this simplified nativity story is on words, sounds, actions, and feelings to which young children can relate. They have had the experience of being tired, of knocking on a door, of sleeping soundly, of hearing a baby cry, of being cared for, and of having visitors. It is difficult for young children to imagine a time that is different from the here and now.

The repetition of main words will help the child anticipate the content of the next group of words. After several readings, a child might like to say the three repeated words before you read the paragraph. Repetition is one important way a child learns.

These repeated words will lend themselves to body movements and the use of sounds. This is an excellent time to involve the whole bodies and minds of the children as they move in appropriate ways and listen for the next clue.

If there are older children in the family or group setting, encourage them to participate, using this simplified story of the birth narrative. They may wish to find the scripture story in Luke 2:1-18 and read it to the family.

As this story is repeated during the pre-Christmas season, add some new dimensions to help the child internalize the events:

1. Talk about the way Joseph and Mary felt as they started their journey, how they felt as they came to the end of the trip. What do you think they said to each other when their son was born? Or when the shepherd visitors came to see them?

2. Give the young child some simple crèche figures that can be moved as the story is read. You may want to introduce one figure each time a story is read, or each person in the family might hold one figure. After the story, suggest that the child move the figures through a sequence of the story, making up the dialogue as the figures are moved.

3. Suggest that the child use the nativity figures with other toys. This provides the child an opportunity to "talk" for the biblical persons, to give the baby Jesus a ride in the baby buggy or wagon, to make a house for the family or a bed for the baby with blocks, or to dress up the baby in tissues or cloth strips. As the child learns to appreciate the holy family in a natural way and to think of Jesus as a friend, the child is laying the groundwork for the acceptance of the greatest gift of all—God's redeeming love through Jesus.

The day had come for Mary and Joseph to leave their home and go to Bethlehem.

There were no buses, no cars, no planes.
So Mary rode on the back of their donkey,
and Joseph walked the whole way.

STEP, STEP, STEP.

The sun went down, and the air began
to get cool. Mary was very tired.
She said to Joseph, "May we stop and ask
at one of the homes for a room for the night?"

KNOCK, KNOCK, KNOCK.

Joseph knocked on the door of a house.
Joseph said to the owner, "Do you have a room
for us to spend the night? We have traveled
a long distance. We are very tired."

NO, NO, NO!

"My whole family is here. There are many children and several out-of-town guests. I have no more room. But I do have a barn in back. You may spend the night there with the animals where it is warm."

WALK, WALK, WALK.

Mary and Joseph went to the barn. They opened
the door. From the light of a small lamp
they could see a large pile of clean hay. Mary
lay down on the soft bed of hay.
Joseph covered her with his warm coat.

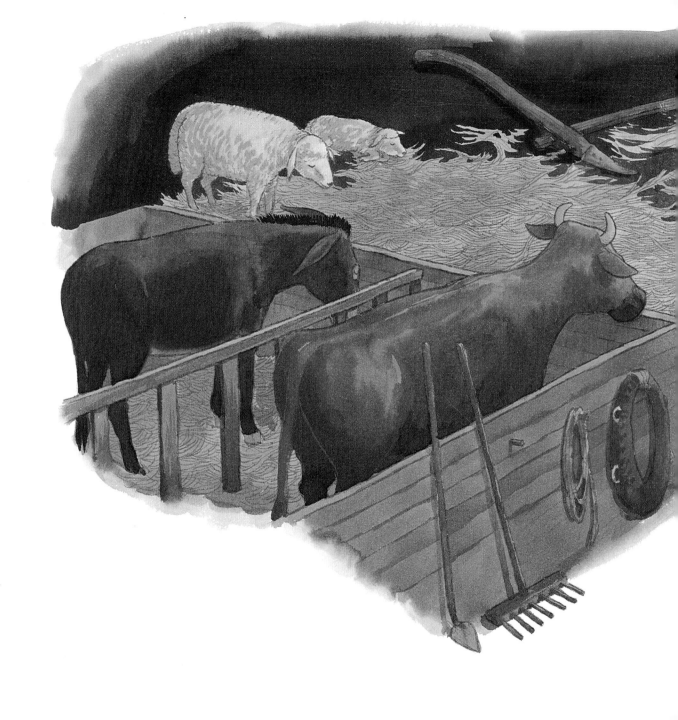

SLEEP, SLEEP, SLEEP.

Mary was very tired. She had been riding all day.
Mary and Joseph went to sleep to the sound
of the animals' breathing and moving in their stalls.
During the night, the time came for Mary to
have her baby.

WAH, WAH, WAH!

The baby gave a loud cry. He was well and strong!
Mary wrapped her baby in soft cloths.
She cuddled him in her arms and fed him.
"Joseph, let's call him Jesus," Mary said.
Mary and Joseph decided the name was good.

ROCK, ROCK, ROCK.

The new mother held her baby. She rocked him in her arms. She cared for him and loved him. The baby needed to sleep. Mary put new hay in the manger. It was Jesus' first bed.

BAA, BAA, BAA.

Shepherds were on the hills. They had gathered their sheep in a large group. It was just like every other night. But as the sheep settled down the shepherds saw a star shining brightly.

They heard some voices say, "Go to Bethlehem and find a very special baby."

GO, GO, GO.

Some of the shepherds left their sheep and went
to Bethlehem to find the baby Jesus.
They walked quickly along the worn path.

SEE, SEE, SEE!

When the shepherds arrived at the barn, they
found the animals, Mary and Joseph, and Jesus.
They had found the very special baby.
This was the beginning of Christmas.